Wolverineology Trivia Challenge

Michigan Wolverines Football

Wolverineology
Trivia
Challenge

Michigan Wolverines Football

Researched by Tom P. Rippey III

Paul F. Wilson & Tom P. Rippey III, Editors

Kick The Ball, Ltd
Lewis Center, Ohio

Trivia by Kick The Ball, Ltd

College Football Trivia

Alabama Crimson Tide	Auburn Tigers	Boston College Eagles	Florida Gators
Georgia Bulldogs	LSU Tigers	Miami Hurricanes	Michigan Wolverines
Nebraska Cornhuskers	Notre Dame Fighting Irish	Ohio State Buckeyes	Oklahoma Sooners
Oregon Ducks	Penn State Nittany Lions	Southern Cal Trojans	Texas Longhorns

Pro Football Trivia

Arizona Cardinals	Baltimore Ravens	Buffalo Bills	Chicago Bears
Cleveland Browns	Dallas Cowboys	Denver Broncos	Green Bay Packers
Indianapolis Colts	Kansas City Chiefs	Minnesota Vikings	New England Patriots
New Orleans Saints	New York Giants	New York Jets	Oakland Raiders
Philadelphia Eagles	Pittsburgh Steelers	San Francisco 49ers	Washington Redskins

Pro Baseball Trivia

Atlanta Braves	Baltimore Orioles	Boston Red Sox	Chicago Cubs
Chicago White Sox	Cincinnati Reds	Detroit Tigers	Houston Astros
Los Angeles Dodgers	Milwaukee Brewers	Minnesota Twins	New York Mets
New York Yankees	Philadelphia Phillies	Saint Louis Cardinals	San Francisco Giants

College Basketball Trivia

Duke Blue Devils	Georgetown Hoyas	Indiana Hoosiers	Kansas Jayhawks
Kentucky Wildcats	Maryland Terrapins	Michigan State Spartans	North Carolina Tar Heels
Syracuse Orange	UConn Huskies	UCLA Bruins	

Pro Basketball Trivia

Boston Celtics	Chicago Bulls	Detroit Pistons	Los Angeles Lakers
Utah Jazz			

Visit **www.TriviaGameBooks.com** for more details.

*This book is dedicated to
Lance Mogdics, Mike Carroll and Kenny Galan,
all are blue through and through.*

**Wolverineology Trivia Challenge: Michigan Wolverines Football;
Fourth Edition 2012**

Published by
Kick The Ball, Ltd
8595 Columbus Pike, Suite 197
Lewis Center, OH 43035
www.TriviaGameBooks.com

Edited by: Paul F. Wilson & Tom P. Rippey III
Designed and Formatted by: Paul F. Wilson
Researched by: Tom P. Rippey III

For information on ordering this book in bulk at reduced prices, please email us at pfwilson@triviagamebooks.com.

International Standard Book Number: 978-1-613320-060-5
Printed and Bound in the United States of America
10 9 8 7 6 5 4 3 2 1

Table of Contents

Dear Friend,

Thank you for purchasing our *Wolverineology Trivia Challenge* game book!

We have made every attempt to verify the accuracy of the questions and answers contained in this book. However it is still possible that from time to time an error has been made by us or our researchers. In the event you find a question or answer that is questionable or inaccurate, we ask for your understanding and thank you for bringing it to our attention so we may improve future editions of this book. Please email us at tprippey@triviagamebooks.com with those observations and comments.

Have fun playing *Wolverineology Trivia Challenge*!

Paul & Tom

Paul Wilson and Tom Rippey
Co-Founders, Kick The Ball, Ltd

PS – You can discover more about all of our current trivia game books by visiting www.TriviaGameBooks.com.

Book Format:

There are four quarters, each made up of fifty questions. Each quarter's questions have assigned point values. Questions are designed to get progressively more difficult as you proceed through each quarter, as well as through the book itself. Most questions are in a four-option multiple-choice format so that you will at least have a 25 percent chance of getting a correct answer for some of the more challenging questions.

We have even added Overtime in the event of a tie, or just in case you want to keep playing a little longer.

Game Options:

One Player -
To play on your own, simply answer each of the questions in all the quarters, and in the overtime section, if you'd like. Use the Player / Team Score Sheet to record your answers and the quarter Answer Keys to check your answers. Calculate each quarter's points and the total for the game at the bottom of the Player / Team Score Sheet to determine your final score.

Two or More Players –
To play with multiple players decide if you will all be competing with each other individually, or if you will form and play as teams. Each player / team will then have its own Player / Team Score Sheet to record its answer. You can use the quarter Answer Keys to check your answers and to calculate your final scores.

How to Play

Wolverineology Trivia Challenge

The Player / Team Score Sheets have been designed so that each team can answer all questions or you can divide the questions up in any combination you would prefer. For example, you may want to alternate questions if two players are playing or answer every third question for three players, etc. In any case, simply record your response to your questions in the corresponding quarter and question number on the Player / Team Score Sheet.

A winner will be determined by multiplying the total number of correct answers for each quarter by the point value per quarter, then adding together the final total for all quarters combined. Play the game again and again by alternating the questions that your team is assigned so that you will answer a different set of questions each time you play.

You Create the Game -
There are countless other ways of using **Wolverineology Trivia Challenge** questions. It is limited only to your imagination. Examples might be using them at your tailgate or other college football related party. Players / Teams who answer questions incorrectly may have to perform a required action, or winners may receive special prizes. Let us know what other games you come up with!

Have fun!

1) Has the Michigan football team ever been known by any other nickname besides "Wolverines"?

Answers begin on page 17

    A) Yes
    B) No

2) What are Michigan's colors?

    A) Black and Gold
    B) White and Blue
    C) Maize and Blue
    D) Yellow and Brown

3) What is the name of the stadium where Michigan plays?

    A) Wolverine Field
    B) Schembechler Stadium
    C) Fielding Field
    D) Michigan Stadium

4) How many Heisman trophy winners played at Michigan?

    A) 1
    B) 2
    C) 3
    D) 5

5) What is the name of the Michigan fight song?

    A) "The Victors"
    B) "Rawhide"
    C) "Hail to the Victors"
    D) "Grease Lightning"

6) What trophy does Michigan and Michigan State play for annually?

    A) Johnny Appleseed Trophy
    B) Paul Bunyan Trophy
    C) Governor's Cup
    D) The Michigan Cup

7) Which ex-President of the United States played center for Michigan?

    A) Ronald Regan
    B) Gerald Ford
    C) Dwight Eisenhower
    D) John F. Kennedy

8) Who had the longest coaching tenure at Michigan?

    A) Fielding Yost
    B) Bennie Oosterbaan
    C) Bo Schembechler
    D) Lloyd Carr

9) Michigan has never had two running backs rush for over 1,000 yards in the same season.

    A) True
    B) False

10) Which Big Ten opponent has Michigan played the most?

    A) Michigan State
    B) Ohio State
    C) Minnesota
    D) Illinois

11) How many times has Michigan appeared in the Rose Bowl?

    A) 13
    B) 15
    C) 17
    D) 20

12) What is the nickname of the stadium where Michigan plays?

    A) The Big House
    B) The Horseshoe
    C) Death Valley
    D) Champions Field

13) What is the name of Michigan's Mascot?

    A) Wolvi the Wolverine
    B) Huggie Bear
    C) Brownie
    D) The team does not have a mascot

14) What trophy does Michigan and Minnesota play for?

    A) Tomahawk Trophy
    B) Little Brown Jug
    C) Great Lakes Award
    D) M State Trophy

15) The stadium seating capacity for Michigan is over 110,000.

    A) Yes
    B) No

16) What year did Michigan play its first-ever game?

    A) 1879
    B) 1885
    C) 1891
    D) 1897

17) How many bowl bound teams did the Wolverines play in 2011?

    A) 4
    B) 6
    C) 8
    D) 10

18) In the song "The Victors," Michigan is champions of what?

    A) The West
    B) The East
    C) The Midwest
    D) The Big Ten

19) Who holds the career rushing record for Michigan?

    A) Tyrone Wheatley
    B) Anthony Thomas
    C) Jamie Morris
    D) Michael Hart

20) Who was the first consensus All-American at Michigan?

    A) William Cunningham
    B) Tom Harmon
    C) Harry Kipke
    D) Desmond Howard

21) What nickname did the Michigan Marching band earn in 1950 after playing in both Yankee Stadium and the Rose Bowl?

    A)   Michigan Pride
    B)   America's Band
    C)   Transcontinental Marching Band
    D)   Band of the Heartland

22) Michigan is a member of the Big Ten's Legends Division.

    A)   True
    B)   False

23) Which of Michigan's head coaches had the most career wins while in Ann Arbor?

    A)   Gary Moeller
    B)   Lloyd Carr
    C)   Bo Schembechler
    D)   Fielding Yost

24) What year was Michigan's first-ever undefeated season (minimum 8 games)?

    A)   1898
    B)   1902
    C)   1910
    D)   1925

25) Who holds the record for the most passing yards in a single game at Michigan?

   A) Jim Harbaugh
   B) John Navarre
   C) Brian Griese
   D) Chad Henne

26) What coach was responsible for the purchase of the Little Brown Jug?

   A) Fielding Yost
   B) Lloyd Carr
   C) Bo Schembechler
   D) Elton Wieman

27) The "wings" on the Michigan helmet were initially painted white.

   A) True
   B) False

28) How many consecutive bowl games has Michigan been to?

   A) 25
   B) 33
   C) 37
   D) 49

29) Have Michigan and Ohio State ever played on a neutral site?

    A) Yes
    B) No

30) Who holds Michigan's record for the most total yards against Ohio State in a single game?

    A) Tim Biakabutuka
    B) John Navarre
    C) Denard Robinson
    D) Tom Brady

31) How many Michigan head coaches have been consensus All-Americans as Michigan football players?

    A) 0
    B) 2
    C) 4
    D) 8

32) Which team has Michigan played the most in bowl games?

    A) Washington
    B) UCLA
    C) Texas
    D) Southern Cal

33) Who received the most individual national awards while at Michigan?

A) Tom Harmon
B) Desmond Howard
C) Charles Woodson
D) David Baas

34) What color were Michigan's helmets prior to 1938?

A) Black
B) Gray
C) Red
D) Blue

35) Who scored the first touchdown for the Wolverines in their 2012 bowl game victory against Virginia Tech?

A) Denard Robinson
B) Martavious Odoms
C) Fitzgerald Toussaint
D) Junior Hemmingway

36) What is Michigan's team MVP Award called?

A) The Yost Award
B) Bo Schembechler Award
C) Maize and Blue Award
D) Best Player Award

37) Michigan has a winning percentage of more than 60 percent against Ohio State.

  A) True
  B) False

38) Against which opponent did the Wolverines score the most points in 2011?

  A) Notre Dame
  B) Nebraska
  C) Minnesota
  D) Purdue

39) What nickname was Coach Herbert Crisler known by?

  A) Crimson
  B) Fritz
  C) The Man in Blue
  D) H-Back Crisler

40) What year did the Michigan band first perform on the football field?

  A) 1898
  B) 1905
  C) 1912
  D) 1923

41) How many AP National Championships has Michigan been awarded?

    A) 2
    B) 3
    C) 5
    D) 7

42) What is Michigan's record for the most consecutive winning seasons?

    A) 21
    B) 29
    C) 35
    D) 40

43) Who was the opponent in the dedication game for the opening of Michigan Stadium?

    A) Ohio State
    B) Navy
    C) Notre Dame
    D) Eastern Michigan

44) All time, how many Big Ten Championships has Michigan won?

    A) 25
    B) 32
    C) 37
    D) 42

45) Who holds the single-game rushing record at Michigan?

A) Tyrone Wheatley
B) Ron Johnson
C) Tim Biakabutuka
D) Tony Boles

46) What year did Michigan have the most consensus All-Americans?

A) 1972
B) 1988
C) 1991
D) 2004

47) How many Michigan head coaches lasted just one season?

A) 2
B) 4
C) 7
D) 11

48) Who holds Michigan's record for the most points scored in a single game?

A) Ron Johnson
B) Tom Harmon
C) Desmond Howard
D) Tyrone Wheatley

49) Excluding QBs, how many Michigan players have been named Rose Bowl MVP?

    A) 1
    B) 3
    C) 5
    D) 7

50) What year did Michigan first celebrate a victory over Ohio State?

    A) 1879
    B) 1892
    C) 1897
    D) 1913

Francis, Albert and Alvin Wistert all played for the Wolverines. All three received consensus All-American honors as tackles (Francis, 1933; Albert, 1942; and Alvin 1948-49). All three wore the same number, #11, which is now retired in their honor. All three have been inducted into the College Football Hall of Fame. Francis never played football before enrolling at Michigan. Albert had his number retired by the Philadelphia Eagles.

1) B – No (The Michigan football team has always been known as the Wolverines. There are only theories as to why, since wolverines are not found in the wild in the state of Michigan.)

2) C – Maize and Blue (A committee of students selected these colors in 1867.)

3) D – Michigan Stadium (It opened in 1927 at a cost of $950,000.)

4) C – 3 (Tom Harmon won the Heisman in 1940, Desmond Howard in 1991 and Charles Woodson in 1997.)

5) A – "The Victors" (Written in 1898, the song is played when the players enter the field and after every Michigan score.)

6) B – Paul Bunyan Trophy (The tradition started in 1953 when former Michigan Governor Gerhard Williams announced he would award a four-foot wooden statue of Paul Bunyan to the winner.)

7) B – Gerald Ford (Ford was voted team MVP in 1934 and also played on the 1932 and 1933 national championship teams.)

8) A – Fielding Yost (25 years, 1901-23, 1925-26)

9) B – False (In 1975 Gordon Bell rushed for 1,390 yards and Rob Little rushed for 1,030 yards; and in 2011 Denard Robinson rushed for 1,176 yards and Fitzgerald Toussaint rushed for 1,041 yards.)

10) B – Ohio State (108 games)

11) D – 20 (UM is second only to Southern Cal, which has 33 appearances.)

12) A – The Big House (Nicknamed due to the fact that Michigan Stadium is the largest non-racing stadium in the United States.)

13) D – The team does not have a mascot (Although Michigan does not have a mascot, two wolverines were taken to a game in 1927, but were considered too ferocious for a return visit.)

14) B – Little Brown Jug (This is the oldest college football trophy game tradition in the Football Bowl Subdivision.)

15) B – No (Even though announced attendance is regularly over 110,000, the official stadium seating capacity is 109,901.)

16) A – 1879 (Michigan defeated the Racine Purple Stockings 1-0 on May 30, 1879.)

17) D – 10 (In 2011, the Wolverines went 8-2 against bowl-bound teams.)

18) A – The West ("Hail! Hail! To Michigan, the champions of the West")

19) D – Michael Hart (Hart gained 5,040 yards on 1,015 attempts for an average of 5.0 yards per carry.)

20) A – William Cunningham (Center, 1898)

21) C – Transcontinental Marching Band

22) A – True (Michigan is in the Legends Division with Iowa, Michigan State, Minnesota, Nebraska and Northwestern.)

23) C – Bo Schembechler (194-48-5 [.796])

24) A – 1898 (10-0)

25) B – John Navarre (He passed for 389 yards versus Iowa in 2003, going 26-49 with one interception and two touchdowns.)

26) A – Fielding Yost (Fearing that Minnesota might contaminate Michigan's drinking water during a game in 1903, Yost sent the team manager to buy a five-gallon jug for water.)

27) B – False (The wings have always been maize. In 1938 Coach Crisler had the "wings" of the Spalding FH5 leather helmets repainted with maize to help players recognize their teammates on the field.)

28) B – 33 (The Wolverines appeared in a bowl game following the regular season from 1975-2007.)

29) B – No

30) D – Tom Brady (1998, 346 total yards; 375 yards passing, -29 yards rushing)
31) B – 2 (Harry Kipke 1922, Bennie Oosterbaan 1925-27)
32) D – Southern Cal (Eight times in the Rose Bowl [2-6])
33) C – Charles Woodson (Woodson received five total awards while at Michigan; Bednarik, Heisman, Thorpe, Nagurski and Walter Camp all in 1997.)
34) A – Black
35) D – Junior Hemmingway (He pulled in a 43-yard touchdown pass from Denard Robinson in the second quarter to give Michigan a 7-6 lead.)
36) B – Bo Schembechler Award (The name was changed from MVP Award to the Bo Schembechler Award in 1995. Tim Biakabutuka was the first recipient, and Denard Robinson won the award in 2011.)
37) B - False (The Wolverines are 58-44-6 against the Buckeyes, for a .565 winning percentage.)
38) C – Minnesota (Michigan beat the Golden Gophers 58-0.)
39) B – Fritz (While playing at the University of Chicago, Coach Amos Alonzo Stagg nicknamed Crisler after the famous violinist Fritz Kreisler.)

40) A – 1898 (The band's first public performance was in 1897. However, its members' first performance on the football field was in 1898.)

41) B – 3 (1947 [awarded after "special" post bowl poll], 1948 and 1997)

42) D – 40 (The Wolverines had winning seasons from 1968-2007.)

43) A – Ohio State (Michigan defeated the Buckeyes 21-0 in the dedication game in 1927.)

44) D – 42 (Michigan last won a Big Ten title in 2004.)

45) B – Ron Johnson (Johnson gained 347 yards on 31 attempts for 11.2 yards per carry versus Wisconsin in 1968.)

46) D – 2004 (Michigan had four consensus All-Americans in 2004: Braylon Edwards, WR; David Baas, OL; Marlin Jackson, DB; and Ernest Shazor, DB.)

47) B – 4 (Murphy Crawford, William Ward, Langdon Lea and George Little)

48) A – Ron Johnson (Johnson recorded five rushing touchdowns versus Wisconsin in 1968 [Michigan 34, Wisconsin 9].)

49) D – 7 (Neil Snow, FB 1902; Robet Chappuis, HB 1948; Donald Dufek, FB 1951; Mel Anthony, FB 1965; Butch Woolfork, RB 1981; Leroy Hoard, FB 1989; and Tyrone Wheatley, RB 1993)

50) C – 1897 (Michigan 34, Ohio State 0)

Note: All answers are valid as of the end of the 2011 season, unless otherwise indicated in the question itself.

1) Where did Brady Hoke coach before Michigan?

Answers begin on page 37

   A) Ball State
   B) LSU
   C) Eastern Michigan
   D) San Diego State

2) What is the first score written on the Little Brown Jug?

   A) 0-0
   B) 0-3
   C) 6-6
   D) 24-7

3) How many Michigan defensive players are in the College Football Hall of Fame?

   A) 0
   B) 1
   C) 3
   D) 6

4) How many decades did the Wolverines win at least 85 games?

   A) 0
   B) 1
   C) 3
   D) 5

5) Which Michigan head coach has the second most all-time wins?

    A)   Bump Elliot
    B)   Harry Kipke
    C)   Lloyd Carr
    D)   Fielding Yost

6) How many undefeated/untied seasons has Michigan had (minimum 8 games)?

    A)   6
    B)   9
    C)   11
    D)   14

7) Who has the most career interceptions for Michigan?

    A)   Tom Curtis
    B)   Charles Woodson
    C)   Tripp Welborne
    D)   Ty Law

8) Which U.S. Service Academy has Michigan never played?

    A)   Air Force
    B)   Navy
    C)   Army
    D)   Has played all three

9) Which coach had the second longest coaching tenure at Michigan?

A) Lloyd Carr
B) Herbert Crisler
C) Bennie Oosterbaan
D) Bo Schembechler

10) Which team has Michigan played fewer than 75 times?

A) Michigan State
B) Illinois
C) Wisconsin
D) Minnesota

11) How many Michigan head coaches have won the team MVP Award as Michigan football players?

A) 0
B) 2
C) 4
D) 6

12) How many Michigan quarterbacks have been named consensus All-American?

A) 0
B) 1
C) 3
D) 4

13) Who scored the first touchdown for Michigan against Ohio State in 2011?

    A) Junior Hemingway
    B) Fitzgerald Toussaint
    C) Denard Robinson
    D) Kevin Koger

14) How many Michigan players have received the team MVP Award more than once?

    A) 1
    B) 3
    C) 5
    D) 7

15) Who holds Michigan's record for the most points scored against Ohio State?

    A) Tim Biakabutuka
    B) Tom Harmon
    C) Chris Perry
    D) Anthony Thomas

16) What are the most sacks recorded in a single season by a Michigan player (since 1980)?

    A) 9
    B) 12
    C) 14
    D) 16

17) Which Michigan player holds the career record for combined punt returns and kickoff returns for touchdowns in Michigan history?

A) Steve Breaston
B) Derrick Alexander
C) Gil Chapman
D) Desmond Howard

18) What is the longest winning streak in the Michigan-Ohio State series?

A) 5
B) 7
C) 9
D) 11

19) When was the most recent season ESPN's *College GameDay* visited Ann Arbor?

A) 2004
B) 2005
C) 2009
D) 2011

20) Does Michigan have a winning record in Bowl games?

A) Yes
B) No

21) When did the "Go Blue, M Club Supports You" banner first appear on the football field at Michigan Stadium?

    A) 1951
    B) 1957
    C) 1962
    D) 1968

22) What year did Michigan first join the Big Ten (then known as the Western Conference)?

    A) 1896
    B) 1904
    C) 1912
    D) 1920

23) What year did Michigan first travel out of state for a game?

    A) 1879
    B) 1883
    C) 1887
    D) 1890

24) Which non-conference team has UM played the most?

    A) Case
    B) Pennsylvania
    C) Chicago
    D) Notre Dame

25) How many Michigan players have won Rose Bowl MVP (includes all positions)?

    A) 7
    B) 10
    C) 12
    D) 15

26) Who holds Michigan's career record for the most points scored?

    A) Anthony Thomas
    B) Tyrone Wheatley
    C) Tom Harmon
    D) Garrett Rivas

27) Which team gave Michigan its largest-ever margin of defeat?

    A) Ohio State
    B) Cornell
    C) Notre Dame
    D) Yale

28) How many Michigan players have been awarded a Bowl MVP twice?

    A) 0
    B) 2
    C) 4
    D) 8

29) Which team does Michigan now face in its annual Big Ten cross-divisional matchup?

   A) Penn State
   B) Illinois
   C) Ohio State
   D) Wisconsin

30) Since fielding its first team in 1879, what year did Michigan not field a team?

   A) 1882
   B) 1886
   C) 1890
   D) 1894

31) Did Tim Biakabutuka have three times as many rushing yards as Heisman Trophy winner Eddie George in the 1995 Michigan-Ohio State game?

   A) Yes
   B) No

32) How many years did Michigan play without a head coach?

   A) 0
   B) 3
   C) 7
   D) 11

33) Did Michigan have a winning record in its first-ever season?

    A) Yes
    B) No

34) Which team gave Michigan its first-ever loss?

    A) Yale
    B) Harvard
    C) Toronto
    D) Chicago

35) What was Michigan's first bowl game other than the Rose Bowl?

    A) Sugar Bowl
    B) Cotton Bowl
    C) Blue Bonnet Bowl
    D) Orange Bowl

36) Who was Michigan's first opponent in Michigan Stadium?

    A) Ohio Wesleyan
    B) Miami, Ohio
    C) Ball State
    D) Florida

37) Who was Michigan's first head coach?

   A) Gustave Ferbert
   B) Mike Murphy
   C) Frank Crawford
   D) Fielding Yost

38) How many three-time consensus All-Americans have played for Michigan?

   A) 1
   B) 3
   C) 5
   D) 7

39) Who is the only Wolverine quarterback to pass for over 3,000 yards in a season?

   A) Tom Brady
   B) Todd Collins
   C) Elvis Grbac
   D) John Navarre

40) Who was the most recent Michigan player to be named consensus All-American two times?

   A) Charles Woodson
   B) Michael Hart
   C) Jake Long
   D) Braylon Edwards

41) Who holds Michigan's record for the most receiving yards in a single game?

    A) Derrick Alexander
    B) Desmond Howard
    C) Jack Clancy
    D) Roy Roundtree

42) Who was the first consensus All-American defensive back at Michigan?

    A) Charles Woodson
    B) Tom Curtis
    C) Ernest Shazor
    D) Tripp Welborne

43) Who had the longest-ever punt return for Michigan against Ohio State?

    A) Steve Breaston
    B) Anthony Carter
    C) Desmond Howard
    D) Tyrone Wheatley

44) What year did Michigan win its first Big Ten title?

    A) 1898
    B) 1913
    C) 1918
    D) 1925

45) Which team did Gary Moeller say was more of a rival to Michigan than Ohio State?

   A) Michigan State
   B) Notre Dame
   C) Illinois
   D) Penn State

46) Which conference opponent does Michigan have the most wins against?

   A) Northwestern
   B) Indiana
   C) Penn State
   D) Minnesota

47) Which Big Ten team has the most wins against Michigan?

   A) Illinois
   B) Michigan State
   C) Ohio State
   D) Minnesota

48) How many Wolverine quarterbacks have thrown at least 25 touchdown passes in a single season?

   A) 1
   B) 2
   C) 4
   D) 5

49) How many Wolverine head coaches have won National Coach of the Year while at Michigan?

    A) 0
    B) 2
    C) 4
    D) 7

50) How many outright Big Ten Championships has Michigan won?

    A) 7
    B) 10
    C) 15
    D) 18

Michigan dropped out of the Big Ten in 1907 because of new league rules limiting games to five per season and allowing only three years varsity status to players. In the 10 years as an independent, Michigan compiled a record of 52-16-7 (.740). The only Big Ten School Michigan played during that period was Minnesota. Michigan won both meetings, 15-6 in 1909 and 6-0 in 1910.

1) D – San Diego State (Hoke coached the Aztecs from 2009-10 posting a 13-12 record [.520].)

2) C – 6-6 (Minnesota had just tied the game with two minutes left when the game was stopped due to the ensuing celebration by the Golden Gophers and their fans.)

3) B – 1 (Tom Curtis, Safety 1967-69, inducted in 2005)

4) C – 3 (Michigan won 96 games in the 1970s, 90 games in the 1980s and 93 games in the 1990s.)

5) D – Fielding Yost (165-29-10 [.833])

6) B – 9 (1898, 1901, 1902, 1904, 1923, 1932, 1947, 1948 and 1997)

7) A – Tom Curtis (22 interceptions from 1967-69)

8) D – Has played all three (Michigan is 4-5 versus Army, 12-5-1 versus Navy, and 1-0 versus Air Force for a combined record of 17-10-1 and .625 winning percentage.)

9) D – Bo Schembechler (21 years, 1969-89)

10) C – Wisconsin (Michigan has played the Badgers 64 times and leads the series 49-14-1 [.773].)

11) B – 2 (Bennie Oosterbaan 1927, Bump Elliot 1947)

12) A – 0 (Stunning considering how many NFL quarterbacks the Wolverines have produced.)

13) C – Denard Robinson (Robinson scored on a 41-yard run on Michigan's second possession.)

14) D – 7 (Denard Robinson [2010-11], Brandon Graham [2008-09], Michael Hart [2006-07], Anthony Carter [1980 and 1982], Ron Johnson [1967-68], Tom Harmon [1939-40] and Ralph Heikkinen [1937-38])

15) B – Tom Harmon (Harmon scored 22 points against the Buckeyes in 1940 [Michigan 40, Ohio State 0].)

16) B – 12 (LaMarr Woodley recorded 12 sacks in 2006, matching the record set by David Bowens in 1996.)

17) A – Steve Breaston (4 punt returns, 1 kickoff return)

18) C – 9 (Michigan from 1901-09)

19) D – 2011 (The College GameDay crew visited Ann Arbor for the game versus Notre Dame, which was the first night game in stadium history.)

20) B – No (Michigan has a 20-21 bowl-game record [.488].)

21) C – 1962 (Bump Elliot allowed the banner on the field for homecoming against Illinois.)

22) A – 1896 (Michigan was a founding member of the conference, but left in 1907 due to conflicts with the Big Ten's decision to limit games played to a total of six per season. They rejoined the conference in 1917.)

23) A – 1879 (Michigan actually traveled to Chicago for that first matchup against Racine.)

24) D – Notre Dame (39 games)

25) B – 10 (Neil Snow FB 1902, Robet Chappuis HB 1948, Donald Dufek FB 1951, Mel Anthony FB 1965, Rick Leach QB 1979, Buthch Woolfork RB 1981, Leroy Hoard FB 1989, Tyrone Wheatley RB 1993, Brian Griese QB 1998 and LaMarr Woodley LB 2005)

26) D – Garrett Rivas (Rivas scored 354 points for the Wolverines from 2003-06.)

27) B – Cornell (In 1889, Cornell handed Michigan its biggest loss in team history [56-0].)

28) C – 4 (Butch Woolfork 1981 Rose Bowl, 1981 Blue Bonnet Bowl; Jamie Morris 1986 Fiesta Bowl, 1988 Hall of Fame Bowl; Tyrone Wheatley 1993 Rose Bowl, 1994 Hall of Fame Bowl; and Anthony Thomas 1999 Citrus Bowl, 2001 Citrus Bowl)

29) C – Ohio State (Michigan is 1-0 in the series since the Big Ten separated into two divisions.)

30) A – 1882

31) A – Yes (Biakabutuka had 313 yards rushing and George had 104 yards rushing.)

32) D – 11 (The Wolverines played without a coach from 1879-90. This does not include 1882 when no team was fielded.)

33) A – Yes (The Wolverines beat Racine and tied Toronto to finish the season 1-0-1.)

34) B – Harvard (Harvard beat the Wolverines 1-0 back when a touchdown counted as one point.)

35) D – Orange Bowl (The Wolverines lost 6-14 to Oklahoma in the 1976 Orange Bowl.)

36) A – Ohio Wesleyan (The Wolverines beat The Fighting Bishops 33-0 in the first game played in Michigan Stadium.)

37) B – Mike Murphy (Murphy was named the first Wolverine head coach in 1891 and was joined midseason by Frank Crawford.)

38) A – 1 (Bennie Oosterbaan, 1925-27)

39) D – John Navarre (Navarre passed for 3,331 yards in 2003; 270-456 with 24 TDs and 10 interceptions.)

40) C – Jake Long (As a Wolverine offensive tackle, Long was a consensus All-American in 2006 and 2007. Michigan has had a total of 12 players named consensus All-American two or more years.)

41) D – Roy Roundtree (He gained 247 yards receiving against Illinois in 2010, breaking a 45-year-old record previously held by Jack Clancy.)

42) B – Tom Curtis (Curtis [S] was named consensus All-American in 1969. He had 49 tackles and 6 INTs.)

43) C – Desmond Howard (Howard struck his famous Heisman pose after returning a punt 93 yards for a touchdown against the Buckeyes in 1991. This is also a school punt return record.)

44) A – 1898 (Michigan finished 3-0 in conference play.)

45) A – Michigan State (Moeller felt that the in-state rivalry meant more to Michigan than the Ohio State game.)

46) D – Minnesota (Michigan has 71 wins against Minnesota to lead the series 71-24-3 [.740].)

47) C – Ohio State (The Buckeyes have 44 wins against the Wolverines, however, Michigan leads the series 58-44-6 [.565].)

48) B – 2 (Chad Henne threw 25 touchdown passes in 2004 and Elvis Grbac threw 25 in 1991.)

49) C – 4 (Fritz Crisler 1947, Bennie Oosterbaan 1948, Bo Schembechler 1969 and Lloyd Carr 1997 [Note: All were awarded the American Football Coaches Association [AFCA] Coach of the Year Award.])

50) D – 18 (1898, 1902, 1925, 1932, 1933, 1947, 1948, 1950, 1964, 1971, 1980, 1982, 1988, 1989, 1991, 1992, 1997 and 2003)

Note: All answers are valid as of the end of the 2011 season, unless otherwise indicated in the question itself.

Wolverineology Trivia Challenge

1) What section of the Michigan band performs a Stepshow on the steps of Revelli Hall before home games?

Answers begin on page 56

   A) Drum line
   B) Trumpet
   C) Saxophone
   D) Flute

2) What year was the first-ever winning season at Michigan (minimum 5 games)?

   A) 1882
   B) 1888
   C) 1899
   D) 1912

3) Against which Big Ten team does Michigan currently have the longest winning streak?

   A) Indiana
   B) Iowa
   C) Northwestern
   D) Penn State

4) What year was the first conference game between Michigan and Ohio State?

   A) 1906
   B) 1912
   C) 1918
   D) 1924

5) What are the most points scored in a game by Michigan?

    A) 90
    B) 110
    C) 130
    D) 150

6) Which Michigan quarterback completed the most passes in a bowl game?

    A) Chris Zurbrugg
    B) Brian Griese
    C) Bob Ptacek
    D) Tom Brady

7) Which non-conference opponent has the most wins against Michigan?

    A) Notre Dame
    B) Southern Cal
    C) Washington
    D) Pennsylvania

8) What is the longest kickoff return by Michigan for a touchdown against Ohio State?

    A) 86 yards
    B) 90 yards
    C) 94 yards
    D) 99 yards

9) Which Wolverine kicker holds the record for the longest field goal in Michigan Stadium?

    A)   Garrett Rivas
    B)   Hayden Epstein
    C)   Adam Finley
    D)   Mike Gilette

10) Twenty Michigan players have recorded 1,000 rushing yards in a season.

    A)   True
    B)   False

11) Who holds Michigan's record for the most yards punting in a season?

    A)   Zoltan Mesko
    B)   Ross Ryan
    C)   Adam Finley
    D)   Jason Vinson

12) Who holds the Michigan record for the most receiving yards in a career?

    A)   Mercury Hayes
    B)   Braylon Edwards
    C)   Tai Streets
    D)   Anthony Carter

13) What is Michigan's record for the most tackles for loss in one season?

    A) 19.5
    B) 23
    C) 28.5
    D) 33

14) When was the first year Michigan played a home game?

    A) 1879
    B) 1881
    C) 1883
    D) 1887

15) What is the largest-ever margin of victory for Michigan against Ohio State?

    A) 35
    B) 42
    C) 69
    D) 86

16) How many points were scored against Fielding Yost's Michigan teams in the 204 games he coached?

    A) 674
    B) 800
    C) 950
    D) 1,324

17) What year did the Snow Bowl take place between Michigan and Ohio State?

    A) 1945
    B) 1950
    C) 1955
    D) 1960

18) The Wolverines have never scored more than 500 points in a season.

    A) True
    B) False

19) All time, how many seasons has Michigan gone undefeated at home?

    A) 35
    B) 41
    C) 49
    D) 55

20) What are the most consecutive wins for Michigan in the Little Brown Jug game?

    A) 5
    B) 8
    C) 13
    D) 16

21) Which Michigan head coach has the highest career winning percentage (min. 3 seasons)?

    A) William Ward
    B) Fielding Yost
    C) Bo Schembechler
    D) Gary Moeller

22) Has Michigan played every Pac 12 team at least once?

    A) Yes
    B) No

23) How many Michigan players are in the College Football Hall of Fame for more than one position?

    A) 0
    B) 2
    C) 4
    D) 6

24) Who was the first consensus All-American wide receiver at Michigan?

    A) Braylon Edwards
    B) Anthony Carter
    C) Desmond Howard
    D) Derrick Alexander

25) What are planted next to Paul Bunyan's feet on the Paul Bunyan trophy?

   A) United States flag and Michigan State flag
   B) Pine trees
   C) Oak trees
   D) UM flag and Michigan State University flag

26) Who was UM's first-ever consensus All-American linebacker?

   A) Mike Taylor
   B) Ron Simpkins
   C) Jarrett Irons
   D) Tom Stincic

27) Who holds the UM season record for receiving yards?

   A) Anthony Carter
   B) David Terrell
   C) Braylon Edwards
   D) Amani Toomer

28) Who was the only Michigan player to receive consensus All-American honors in the 1950s?

   A) Ron Kramer
   B) Bill Yearby
   C) Dan Dierdorf
   D) Jim Mandich

29) Has a Michigan quarterback ever passed for over 10,000 yards in a career?

    A) Yes
    B) No

30) What is the winning percentage of coaches that lasted one season or less at Michigan?

    A) .497
    B) .566
    C) .633
    D) .716

31) Who holds Michigan's record for the most points scored in a season?

    A) Desmond Howard
    B) Anthony Thomas
    C) Anthony Carter
    D) Chris Perry

32) How many times have Michigan players finished second in the Heisman voting?

    A) 2
    B) 3
    C) 5
    D) 6

33) How many times has Michigan finished last in the Big Ten?

    A) 2
    B) 4
    C) 6
    D) 8

34) How many years did Tom Harmon lead the nation in all-purpose yards?

    A) 0
    B) 1
    C) 2
    D) 3

35) What are the most consecutive Big Ten titles Michigan has won?

    A) 3
    B) 5
    C) 6
    D) 9

36) What is UM's record for the most consecutive bowl game losses?

    A) 2 games
    B) 5 games
    C) 7 games
    D) 9 games

37) How many losses did Michigan have going into the historic 1969 game versus No. 1 ranked Ohio State?

   A) 1
   B) 2
   C) 4
   D) 5

38) What was the name of Michigan's first home field?

   A) Regents Field
   B) Ann Arbor Fairgrounds
   C) Tiger Stadium
   D) Wayne County Fairgrounds

39) How many times has Michigan shut out an opponent?

   A) 235
   B) 287
   C) 327
   D) 342

40) Since 1948, what is Michigan's longest drought between bowl appearances?

   A) 1 year
   B) 5 years
   C) 9 years
   D) 13 years

41) What are the most consecutive bowl games Michigan has won?

    A) 2
    B) 4
    C) 6
    D) 9

42) Who is the oldest college football player to be named consensus All-American?

    A) Alvin Wistert
    B) Bill Yearby
    C) Marlin Jackson
    D) Jim Elliot

43) How many combined rushing and passing yards did Michigan have in the Snow Bowl?

    A) 27
    B) 41
    C) 52
    D) 60

44) Who coached Michigan in their first Big Ten season?

    A) Langdon Lea
    B) Fielding Yost
    C) William Ward
    D) Bump Elliot

45) Who was the first-ever conference opponent for Michigan?

   A) Minnesota
   B) Chicago
   C) Indiana
   D) Purdue

46) How many Michigan players have been named first team Academic All-American?

   A) 18
   B) 20
   C) 23
   D) 28

47) Where did Michigan play before Michigan Stadium?

   A) Regents Field
   B) Ferry Field
   C) Maize Stadium
   D) Ann Arbor Fairgrounds

48) What is Michigan's longest drought between Big Ten Championships?

   A) 7 years
   B) 9 years
   C) 11 years
   D) 13 years

49) Who was Michigan's 800th all-time win against?

A) Ohio State
B) Northwestern
C) Central Michigan
D) Wisconsin

50) The Wolverines rushed for more than 2,500 yards as a team in 2011.

A) True
B) False

Wolverineology Trivia Challenge

Up until 1901, many of the Wolverines' big games were played on the field of the Detroit Athletic Club to accommodate all of the alumni who wanted to see their team in action. Michigan's 1895 game against Minnesota, which Michigan won 20-0, was held at the Detroit Baseball Park. The last game played there was in 1901. That game ended in a Wolverine win against Carlisle (Michigan 22, Carlisle 0).

1) A – Drum line (The drum line performs on the steps of Revelli Hall about 90 minutes before each home game.)

2) B – 1888 (The Wolverines finished the season 4-1.)

3) A – Indiana (Michigan has beaten the Hoosiers 17 straight meetings and leads the overall series 52-9 [.852].)

4) C – 1918 (Michigan left the Big Ten in 1907 and did not rejoin until 1917. Ohio State was not a member until 1913.)

5) C – 130 (In 1904 Michigan beat West Virginia 130-0.)

6) D – Tom Brady (Brady completed 34 passes against Alabama in the 2000 Orange Bowl [Michigan 35, Alabama 34].)

7) A – Notre Dame (The Irish have 15 wins against UM; Michigan leads the series 23-15-1 [.603].)

8) B – 90 yards (Dave Raimey, 1961)

9) D – Mike Gilette (Gilette kicked a 53-yarder versus Iowa on Oct. 18, 1986.)

10) B – False (Nineteen players have rushed for 1,000 yards in a season a combined 31 times.)

11) A – Zoltan Mesko (Mesko punted 80 times for 3,436 yards in 2008.)

12) B – Braylon Edwards (Edwards gained 3,541 receiving yards on 252 receptions, with 39 touchdowns from 2001-04.)

13) C – 28.5 (Shawn Crable, 2007)

14) C – 1883 (The Wolverines did not have a home game until their fourth season of play.)

15) D – 86 (Michigan beat the Buckeyes 86-0 in 1902.)

16) B – 800 (That's only 3.9 points given up per game!)

17) B – 1950 (The Snow Bowl was played in blizzard conditions, with the game deciding the Big Ten Rose Bowl representative that season. The Wolverines won even though they did not gain a first down in the game [Michigan 9, Ohio State 3].)

18) B – False (Michigan scored a total of 644 points in 1902 [58.5 per game average]. The closest the Wolverines have gotten since then is 460 points in 2003.)

19) D – 55 (The last time was in 2011.)

20) D – 16 (Michigan won every meeting from 1987 through 2004.)

21) C – Bo Schembechler (143-24-3, .850)

22) A – Yes (Michigan has an overall record of 48-23-1 against current Pac 12 teams [.674].)

23) B – 2 (Merv Pregulman for tackle and center; Neil Snow for end and fullback.)

24) B – Anthony Carter (Carter was first named consensus All-American in 1981. For the season, he had 50 receptions for 952 yards and eight touchdowns. Carter was also consensus All-American in 1982 with 43 receptions for 844 yards and eight TDs.)

25) D – UM flag and Michigan State University flag

26) A – Mike Taylor (He was named consensus All-American in 1971 after recording 97 tackles, seven pass breakups and two interceptions.)

27) C – Braylon Edwards (He gained 1,330 receiving yards in 2004.)

28) A – Ron Kramer (Kramer was twice named consensus All-American in the 1950s as an end. In 1955 Kramer had 12 receptions for 224 yards and four touchdowns; in 1956 Kramer had 18 receptions for 353 yards and two touchdowns.)

29) B – No (Chad Henne came the closest with 9,715 yards over his career.)

30) D – .716 (One-year head coaches finished a combined 26-10-1.)

31) A – Desmond Howard (Howard reached the end zone 23 times in 1991 [two rushing, 19 receiving, one kickoff return and one punt return] for a total of 138 points.)

32) A – 2 (Tom Harmon in 1939 [winner was Nile Kinnick from Iowa] and Bob Chappuis in 1947 [winner was John Lujack from Notre Dame].)

33) B – 4 (1934, 1936, 1962 and 2009)

34) C – 2 (1939 1,208 yards; 1940 1,312 yards)

35) B – 5 (1988-92)

36) C – 7 games (1970 and 1972 Rose Bowls; 1976 Orange Bowl; 1977-79 Rose Bowls; and 1979 Gator Bowl)

37) B – 2 (The Wolverines had previous losses to No. 7 Missouri and unranked Michigan State.)
38) B – Ann Arbor Fairgrounds
39) D – 342 (The last time was in 2011 against Minnesota [Michigan 58, Minnesota 0].)
40) D – 13 years (The Wolverines did not participate in a bowl game from 1952-64.)
41) B – 4 (This has happened twice in team history, most recently in bowl games played following the 1997-2000 seasons.)
42) A – Alvin Wistert (He played tackle for the Wolverines and was named consensus All-American in 1948-49. Wistert was 33 years old in 1949.)
43) A – 27 (The Wolverines had zero yards passing on nine attempts and 27 yards rushing. The top rusher for Michigan was Ralph Stratton with 14 yards on 12 carries.)
44) C – William Ward (Michigan finished 2-1 the first Big Ten season.)
45) D – Purdue (Michigan beat Purdue 16-0 in the school's first-ever conference game in 1896.)
46) A – 18 (The last player to be named first team Academic All-American was punter Zoltan Mesko in 2009.)
47) B – Ferry Field (The Wolverines played on Ferry Field from 1902-26.)
48) D – 13 years (Michigan did not win a Big Ten Championship from 1951-63.)

49) D – Wisconsin (Michigan recorded its 800th victory at home against the Badgers on Sept. 30, 2000 [Michigan 13, Wisconsin 10].)

50) A – True (Michigan rushed for 2,884 yards.)

Note: All answers are valid as of the end of the 2011 season, unless otherwise indicated in the question itself.

1) What is the longest win streak for either Michigan or Michigan State in the Paul Bunyan Game?

Answers begin on page 75

    A) 4
    B) 6
    C) 8
    D) 10

2) How many former Michigan players have been inducted into the Pro Football Hall of Fame?

    A) 5
    B) 7
    C) 9
    D) 12

3) How many teams does Michigan have at least 50 wins against?

    A) 3
    B) 4
    C) 6
    D) 8

4) Has Michigan ever had three players rush for 100 yards in the same game?

    A) Yes
    B) No

5) How many jersey numbers has Michigan retired?

  A) 5
  B) 6
  C) 8
  D) 9

6) What is the largest margin of victory for Michigan over Notre Dame?

  A) 14 points
  B) 38 points
  C) 52 points
  D) 65 points

7) Excluding Michigan State, who is the last school from Michigan to beat the Wolverines?

  A) Albion
  B) Eastern Michigan
  C) Kalamazoo
  D) No team

8) How many former Michigan head coaches are in the College Football Hall of Fame?

  A) 2
  B) 4
  C) 6
  D) 7

9) What number did Bo Schembechler make the scout team wear before the Ohio State game in 1969?

    A) No number
    B) 1
    C) 50
    D) 99

10) When was the last time Michigan was shut out?

    A) 1984
    B) 1990
    C) 1996
    D) 2002

11) Under which coach was Michigan's record set for the most consecutive conference wins?

    A) Fielding Yost
    B) Fritz Crisler
    C) Bo Schembechler
    D) Gary Moeller

12) How many shutouts did Michigan have under Coach Fielding Yost?

    A) 73
    B) 93
    C) 113
    D) 133

13) What decade did Michigan have the highest winning percentage?

    A) 1900s
    B) 1910s
    C) 1940s
    D) 1970s

14) Who holds Michigan's single-season rushing record?

    A) Tim Biakabutuka
    B) Anthony Thomas
    C) Tony Boles
    D) Ricky Powers

15) Which team has Michigan played the most to open the season?

    A) Michigan State
    B) Case
    C) Eastern Michigan
    D) Miami (Ohio)

16) Who was the first opponent to draw over 100,000 fans into Michigan Stadium?

    A) Ohio State
    B) Notre Dame
    C) Indiana
    D) Michigan State

17) What were the names of the two live wolverines that were on display for Michigan Stadium's dedication in 1927?

    A) Bennie and Biff
    B) Spartan and Buckeye eaters
    C) Tom and Jerry
    D) Abbott and Costello

18) How many points did Michigan score in the fourth quarter against Minnesota in 2003?

    A) 21
    B) 28
    C) 31
    D) 35

19) Brady Hoke led the Wolverines to wins against Notre Dame, Michigan State and Ohio State in his first season as Michigan's head coach.

    A) True
    B) False

20) Who has the most receptions for Michigan in a single game against Ohio State?

    A) Brad Myers
    B) Braylon Edwards
    C) Marquise Walker
    D) Tai Streets

21) All time, how many head coaches has Michigan had?

    A) 12
    B) 14
    C) 16
    D) 18

22) What are the most consecutive losses for Michigan in the Little Brown Jug game?

    A) 3
    B) 7
    C) 9
    D) 12

23) Which coach has the second highest winning percentage at Michigan (min. 3 seasons)?

    A) Fielding Yost
    B) Lloyd Carr
    C) Bump Elliot
    D) Bennie Oosterbaan

24) Does Michigan have more than a .750 all-time winning percentage in Big Ten play?

    A) Yes
    B) No

25) Since 1956, why does Michigan Stadium's seating capacity always end in the number 1?

    A)   Indicates first place in stadium size
    B)   One seat is always left for Coach Fritz Crisler
    C)   The top row always has to end in an odd number
    D)   Signifies the quest to be the best

26) What is Michigan's all-time win total?

    A)   869
    B)   873
    C)   884
    D)   895

27) Which Wolverine holds the Rose Bowl record for the most touchdowns and points scored in a single game?

    A)   Neil Snow
    B)   Tyrone Wheatley
    C)   Chris Perry
    D)   Bob Westfall

28) How many Michigan players have won the Outland Trophy?

    A)   0
    B)   1
    C)   3
    D)   5

29) What decade did Michigan have the lowest winning percentage?

    A) 1930s
    B) 1950s
    C) 1960s
    D) 1990s

30) What is the largest-ever margin of victory for Michigan in a bowl game?

    A) 19 points
    B) 29 points
    C) 39 points
    D) 49 points

31) How many Michigan players are in the College Football Hall of Fame?

    A) 25
    B) 29
    C) 32
    D) 36

32) What position did Brady Hoke play in college?

    A) Linebacker
    B) Tackle
    C) Tight End
    D) Defensive Back

33) How many decades has Michigan won at least 80 percent of its games?

   A) 0
   B) 1
   C) 3
   D) 5

34) What team gave Michigan its largest-ever margin of defeat in a bowl game?

   A) Southern Cal
   B) Mississippi State
   C) Washington
   D) BYU

35) Who holds the Rose Bowl rushing record for Michigan?

   A) Tyrone Wheatley
   B) Leroy Hoard
   C) Chris Perry
   D) Anthony Thomas

36) How many times has Michigan appeared in the Orange/Sugar/Fiesta/Rose bowls combined?

   A) 15
   B) 22
   C) 25
   D) 29

37) What was the highest winning percentage of a Michigan head coach that lasted only one season?

    A) .525
    B) .650
    C) .775
    D) .900

38) How many years did Michigan play a doubleheader to open the season?

    A) Never
    B) 1
    C) 3
    D) 5

39) How many Michigan linebackers have won a bowl MVP?

    A) 0
    B) 1
    C) 3
    D) 5

40) How many Michigan players have won the Lombardi Award?

    A) 1
    B) 2
    C) 4
    D) 5

41) What is Michigan's record for the most consecutive games without a loss?

    A) 11
    B) 26
    C) 41
    D) 56

42) How many seasons did Elvis Grbac lead the nation in passing efficiency?

    A) 0
    B) 1
    C) 2
    D) 3

43) Which Michigan player received the most individual national awards in a single year?

    A) Charles Woodson
    B) Tom Harmon
    C) Desmond Howard
    D) Erick Anderson

44) All time, how many wins does Michigan have at Michigan Stadium?

    A) 384
    B) 392
    C) 401
    D) 413

45) How many first round NFL Draft picks has Michigan produced?

    A) 35
    B) 39
    C) 43
    D) 50

46) Did Lloyd Carr ever win Big Ten Coach of the Year?

    A) Yes
    B) No

47) How many Michigan players have been selected as Big Ten Freshman of the Year?

    A) 1
    B) 3
    C) 4
    D) 6

48) What is the Michigan record for the most consecutive wins without a tie?

    A) 29
    B) 35
    C) 41
    D) 59

49) What is the only defensive category in which the 1997 Michigan Wolverines did not lead the nation?

    A) Scoring defense
    B) Total defense
    C) Passing defense
    D) Rushing defense

50) How many Michigan coaches and players are in the Rose Bowl Hall of Fame?

    A) 3
    B) 5
    C) 7
    D) 9

In 1940, Tom Harmon bookended the season with spectacular performances. In the season opener against California he ran back the opening kickoff for a touchdown, returned a punt for a touchdown, had two rushing touchdowns and a passing touchdown. As if this were not enough, he kicked four extra points. In the final game of the season at Ohio State, Harmon threw two passing touchdowns, ran for three touchdowns and kicked four extra points. He also punted three times for an average of 50 yards per punt, and had three interceptions on defense. These performances helped earn him a well deserved Heisman Trophy.

1) C – 8 (Michigan won every meeting from 1970-77.)

2) B – 7 (Benny Friedman was inducted in 2005, George Allen in 2002, Tom Mack in 1999, Dan Dierdorf in 1996, Len Ford in 1976, Bill Hewitt in 1971 and Elroy Hirsh in 1968.)

3) C – 6 (Ohio State 58, Michigan State 67, Minnesota 71, Illinois 68, Northwestern 53 and Indiana 52)

4) A – Yes (Gordon Bell [100 yards], Rob Lytle [106 yards] and Harlan Huckleby [157 yards] each had a 100-yard game on the ground against Northwestern on Oct. 18, 1975 [Michigan 69, Northwestern 0].)

5) A – 5 (#11 for the Wistert brothers, Tom Harmon's #98, Ron Kramer's #87, Gerald Ford's #48 and Bennie Oosterbaan's #47)

6) B – 38 points (The Wolverines have beaten the Irish two times [2003, 2007] by 38 points.)

7) D – No team (Other than the Spartans, no team from Michigan has ever beaten the Wolverines.)

8) C – 6 (Fielding Yost, George Little, Tad Wieman, Fritz Crisler, Bo Schembechler and Lloyd Carr)

9) C – 50 (Schembechler made the scout team wear this number to constantly remind the players of the 50 points scored against them by Ohio State in 1968.)

10) A – 1984 (The Wolverines were shut out in Iowa 0-26. Michigan has only been shut out a total of 75 times in school history.)

11) D – Gary Moeller (Michigan won 19 consecutive Big Ten wins under Moeller from 1990-92.)

12) C – 113 (That's 55.4 percent of his 204 games coached.)

13) A – 1900s (82-8-3, .898)

14) A – Tim Biakabutuka (He gained 1,818 yards in 1995 on 303 carries with 12 touchdowns.)

15) B – Case (Played in 16 season openings, last meeting in 1923; Michigan's record in those season openers is 15-0-1.)

16) D – Michigan State (In 1956 over 100,000 fans filled Michigan Stadium for the first time [Michigan 0, Michigan State 9].)

17) A – Bennie and Biff (The wolverines were on loan from the Detroit Zoo, but it was decided these animals were too ferocious to keep. However, while Bennie was returned, Biff was kept at the University of Michigan Zoo for students to visit.)

18) C – 31 (Michigan scored 31 points in the fourth quarter to win 38-35 at Minnesota.)

19) B – False (Michigan 35, Notre Dame 31; Michigan 40, Ohio State 34; and Michigan 14, Michigan State 28)

20) C – Marquise Walker (He had 15 receptions in 2001 for 160 yards and two touchdowns. Walker's reception total matched his Wolverine record-setting game against Washington earlier in the season.)

21) D – 18

22) C – 9 (Michigan lost the trophy game from 1934-42.)

23) B – Lloyd Carr (75-21, .781)

24) B – No (The Wolverines are 473-185-18 all time in conference play for a .713 winning percentage.)

25) B – One seat is always left for Coach Fritz Crisler (This tradition started in 1956 with the location of the seat remaining a secret.)

26) D – 895 (The Wolverines all-time record is 895-310-36 for a .736 winning percentage. These are also the most wins of any college football program regardless of division.)

27) A – Neil Snow (Snow scored five touchdowns against Stanford in the 1902 Rose Bowl. Back then touchdowns counted as five points. His 25 point total still holds as a Rose Bowl scoring record.)

28) A – 0

29) C – 1960s (55-40-2, .577)

30) D – 49 points (On two occasions: 1902 Rose Bowl [Michigan 49, Stanford 0]; and the 1948 Rose Bowl [Michigan 49, Southern Cal 0])

31) B – 29 (Desmond Howard is the most recent Wolverine inducted into the College Football Hall of Fame [2010].)

32) A – Linebacker (Hoke lettered four years at Ball State from 1977-80. He was team captain in 1980 and earned All-MAC Second Team honors.)

33) C – 3 (1900s, 82-8-3 .898; 1940s 74-15-3 .821; 1970s 96-16-3 .848)

34) B – Mississippi State (The Wolverines lost by 38 points to the Bulldogs in the 2011 Gator Bowl [Michigan 14, Mississippi State 52].)

35) A – Tyrone Wheatley (He gained 235 yards in 1993 on 15 carries and three touchdowns. He was 12 yards from tying the Rose Bowl record of 247 yards set by Charles White of Southern Cal, but had to leave the game early due to cramps.)

36) C – 25 (20 Rose Bowls, two Orange Bowls, two Sugar Bowls and one Fiesta Bowl)

37) D – .900 (William Ward, 1896, 9-1)

38) C – 3 (Michigan played doubleheaders in 1929-31 and went 6-0 in those games, outscoring opponents 156-6.)

39) B – 1 (Sam Sword, 1999 Citrus Bowl [Michigan 45, Arkansas 31])

40) A – 1 (LaMarr Woodley, 2006)

41) D – 56 (From Sept. 28, 1901, until Nov. 25, 1905; all under Coach Fielding Yost. The Wolverines went 55-0-1 during this stretch.)

42) C – 2 (1991, 169.0 rating, 1,955 yards, 24 touchdowns, five interceptions, and .667 completion percentage; 1992, 154.2 rating, 1,465 yards, 15 touchdowns, 12 interceptions, and .663 completion percentage)

43) A – Charles Woodson (1997, Bednarik, Heisman, Thorpe, Nagurski and Walter Camp)

44) B – 392 (The Wolverines are 392-120-15 all time at Michigan Stadium for a winning percentage of .758.)

45) C – 43 (The last Michigan player selected in the first round of the NFL Draft was Brandon Graham in the 2010 draft. The Eagles selected him 13th overall.)

46) B – No (Lloyd Carr was never named Big Ten Coach of the Year. Joe Tiller from Purdue won in 1997, the year the Wolverines won the national title.)

47) C – 4 (Charles Woodson in 1995 by the coaches, Anthony Thomas in 1997 by the coaches and media, Steve Breaston in 2003 by the coaches and Michael Hart in 2004 by the coaches and media.)

48) A – 29 (Fielding Yost's teams won 29 straight without a tie from 1901-03.)

49) D – Rushing defense (The 1997 team led the nation in scoring defense, 8.9 points per game; total defense, 206.9 yards per game; and passing defense with a rating of 75.8 and 116 ypg giving up only four passing touchdowns with 22 interceptions.)

50) C – 7 (Mel Anthony, Butch Woofolk, Bo Schembechler, Bob Chappuis, Neil Snow, Bump Elliot and Chuck Ortmann)

Note: All answers are valid as of the end of the 2011 season, unless otherwise indicated in the question itself.

1) How many consecutive games have 100,000 or more fans attended a Wolverine game at Michigan Stadium?

Answers begin on page 83

  A) 179
  B) 195
  C) 210
  D) 238

2) How many times has Michigan begun the season ranked No. 1 in the first AP poll?

  A) 1
  B) 3
  C) 5
  D) 7

3) What year were the most individual national honors awarded to Michigan players?

  A) 1994
  B) 1997
  C) 2003
  D) 2006

4) Who is the most recent Michigan coach to be named Big Ten Coach of the Year?

  A) Gary Moeller
  B) Bo Schembechler
  C) Brady Hoke
  D) Lloyd Carr

5) How many Wolverines have been picked No. 1 overall in the NFL Draft?

    A) 1
    B) 2
    C) 4
    D) 5

6) Denard Robinson was named Big Ten Player of the Year his freshman season.

    A) True
    B) False

7) What are the most consecutive years the Michigan-Ohio State game decided who would go to the Rose Bowl?

    A) 5
    B) 7
    C) 8
    D) 10

8) Which game did Fritz Crisler say was the greatest upset he had ever seen?

    A) UM victory over Cal in the 1951 Rose Bowl
    B) UM victory over No. 1 ranked Ohio State in 1969
    C) UM loss to unranked Purdue in 1976
    D) UM loss to unranked Wisconsin in 1981

9) Which non-conference opponent does Michigan have the most wins against?

    A) Notre Dame
    B) UCLA
    C) Case
    D) Chicago

10) Which Michigan coach was the first in college football to use motion as a decoy?

    A) Harry Kipke
    B) Fritz Crisler
    C) Fielding Yost
    D) Elton Wieman

1) D – 238 (The streak began in a game against Purdue on Nov. 8, 1975 [Michigan 28, Purdue 0].)

2) B – 3 (1949, 1981 and 1989)

3) B – 1997 (All were won by Charles Woodson: Bednarik, Heisman, Thorpe, Nagurski and Walter Camp.)

4) C – Brady Hoke (He was named Big Ten Coach of the Year in 2011 after leading the Wolverines to an 11-2 season.)

5) B – 2 (Tom Harmon was drafted No. 1 overall by the Bears in 1941 and Jake Long was the top draft pick in 2008 by the Dolphins.)

6) A – True (Both the media and coaches selected Robinson as Big Ten Player of the Year.)

7) D – 10 (Michigan-Ohio State decided the Rose Bowl representative every year from 1972-81.)

8) B – UM victory over No. 1 ranked Ohio State in 1969

9) C – Case (UM leads the series 26-0-1 [.981].)

10) C – Fielding Yost

Note: All answers are valid as of the end of the 2011 season, unless otherwise indicated in the question itself.

Player / Team Score Sheet

Name:_____

First Quarter		Second Quarter		Third Quarter		Fourth Quarter		Overtime Bonus	
1	26	1	26	1	26	1	26	1	
2	27	2	27	2	27	2	27	2	
3	28	3	28	3	28	3	28	3	
4	29	4	29	4	29	4	29	4	
5	30	5	30	5	30	5	30	5	
6	31	6	31	6	31	6	31	6	
7	32	7	32	7	32	7	32	7	
8	33	8	33	8	33	8	33	8	
9	34	9	34	9	34	9	34	9	
10	35	10	35	10	35	10	35	10	
11	36	11	36	11	36	11	36		
12	37	12	37	12	37	12	37		
13	38	13	38	13	38	13	38		
14	39	14	39	14	39	14	39		
15	40	15	40	15	40	15	40		
16	41	16	41	16	41	16	41		
17	42	17	42	17	42	17	42		
18	43	18	43	18	43	18	43		
19	44	19	44	19	44	19	44		
20	45	20	45	20	45	20	45		
21	46	21	46	21	46	21	46		
22	47	22	47	22	47	22	47		
23	48	23	48	23	48	23	48		
24	49	24	49	24	49	24	49		
25	50	25	50	25	50	25	50		
___x 1 =____		___x 2 =____		___x 3 =____		___x 4 =____		___x 4 =____	

Multiply total number correct by point value/quarter to calculate totals for each quarter.

Add total of all quarters below.

Total Points:_____

Thank you for playing *Wolverineology Trivia Challenge*.

Additional score sheets are available at:
www.TriviaGameBooks.com

85

Player / Team Score Sheet

Name:_____

First Quarter			Second Quarter			Third Quarter			Fourth Quarter			Overtime Bonus	
1	26		1	26		1	26		1	26		1	
2	27		2	27		2	27		2	27		2	
3	28		3	28		3	28		3	28		3	
4	29		4	29		4	29		4	29		4	
5	30		5	30		5	30		5	30		5	
6	31		6	31		6	31		6	31		6	
7	32		7	32		7	32		7	32		7	
8	33		8	33		8	33		8	33		8	
9	34		9	34		9	34		9	34		9	
10	35		10	35		10	35		10	35		10	
11	36		11	36		11	36		11	36			
12	37		12	37		12	37		12	37			
13	38		13	38		13	38		13	38			
14	39		14	39		14	39		14	39			
15	40		15	40		15	40		15	40			
16	41		16	41		16	41		16	41			
17	42		17	42		17	42		17	42			
18	43		18	43		18	43		18	43			
19	44		19	44		19	44		19	44			
20	45		20	45		20	45		20	45			
21	46		21	46		21	46		21	46			
22	47		22	47		22	47		22	47			
23	48		23	48		23	48		23	48			
24	49		24	49		24	49		24	49			
25	50		25	50		25	50		25	50			
___ x 1 = ___			___ x 2 = ___			___ x 3 = ___			___ x 4 = ___			___ x 4 = ___	

Multiply total number correct by point value/quarter to calculate totals for each quarter.

Add total of all quarters below.

Total Points:_____

Thank you for playing *Wolverineology Trivia Challenge*.

Additional score sheets are available at:
www.TriviaGameBooks.com